CAPRICORN

EARTH

The earth the air the water and the fire
Then 'gan to range themselves in huge array
And with contrary forces to conspire
Each against other by all means they may.

EDMUND SPENSER, *Hymn of Love*

The Elizabethans fully appreciated the poet's fears at the prospect of chaos in Nature's law. Their own longing for order was no less real than ours. Yet like our own times, the world in which they lived was becoming increasingly difficult to control and regulate. Nothing could or ever would, however, be the same, for them, after the astonishing events of 1588.

Europe was dominated by the might of imperial Spain. On land, its armies had carried the crusading spirit of the counter-Reformation from Italy to the Baltic shores. The huge Portuguese empire had been annexed, subjugated. At sea, the Spanish fleet controlled the Mediterranean, the Atlantic and the Pacific. The tense strands of the net stretched across continents, and over this vast empire one man ruled supreme: Philip II of Spain.

France, then boiling with internal feuds, he could afford to ignore; the rebellious Netherlands, reeling beneath the blows of his brilliant general, the Duke of Parma, must soon be his entirely; only England, traditional mistress of the narrow seas, stood in the path of total supremacy.

King Philip II of Spain now seems an unlikely precursor to such would-be world conquerors as Napoleon, or Adolf Hitler, yet he shared their unmistakable fanatical fervour. Shut up like a hermit in the Escorial Palace, near Madrid, Philip was dedicated to prayer, and the administration of his huge Empire. No affair of state was too trivial to command his attention; no campaign too mean to concentrate his consuming mind; no matter on Spain's, or the Holy Church's behalf, too minor to engage his wholehearted interest. In his spidery handwriting, from the centre of this vast, spiralling web, Philip II controlled the destinies of kingdoms and men. Yet still he lusted for more.

In 1554, as a dapper twenty-seven year-old, he had come to England to marry. His bride, Queen Mary, step-sister to Elizabeth, at thirty-eight had failed to produce an heir. What little he had seen of Elizabeth, he had liked. He had waited, and wondered, sometimes anxiously, in the thirty years following her coronation if this politely cool and enigmatic Englishwoman would take a husband. The time for such reflection was now past. Philip, a martyr to gout and insomnia, was no longer in any mood to be further duped by this

Capricorn – Astrological Earth sign. The carved heads used to decorate each chapter opening in this book are taken from the panelled room at Buckland Abbey, home of Sir Francis Drake.

KING PHILIP II OF SPAIN

King Philip of Spain.

'Being a king is nothing but a kind of slavery that carries a crown.'

Philip acceded to the Spanish crown in 1556 at the age of 28. He saw his kingship as ordained by God and applied himself with a priest-like dedication to imposing God's will, as he saw it, to the governance and expansion of his far-flung empire.

As a Prince he married Mary I of England – in an attempt to strengthen Anglo-Spanish relations. However, Mary's relentless persecution of Protestants failed to achieve harmony. Following her death in 1558, Philip, now King of Spain, unsuccessfully offered marriage to Mary's half-sister Elizabeth.

Inevitably, the schism between Protestant and Catholic and the clash between the growth of Spain's empire and England's own enterprises abroad led to conflict and finally to war, with Philip determining upon invasion of England as the final solution.

Increasingly bigoted and morose following the defeat of the Armada in 1588, he nevertheless continued to plan further invasions of England. Unsuccessful, and responsible for a decline in Spanish power, Philip died in 1598.

ELIZABETH I

Queen Elizabeth I, from a portrait by Zucchero.

'I am a lion's cub and I have a lion's heart.'

Elizabeth succeeded her sister, Mary, to the Tudor throne in 1558, a determined young woman of 25. Her realm was in a shambles and she resolved to rebuild it, to restore the treasury, re-establish the Church, and to build up the navy in readiness to defend England and to forge an empire.

From the first she was popular with her people and found loyalty in her ministers and statesmen. In an age of adventurers she found in her countrymen an abundance of brave and capable soldiers and mariners from whom she exacted great loyalty and respect: Hawkyns, Ralegh, Howard, Walsingham, Drake, the Gilberts, the Cecils, and many besides.

It was such men that helped Elizabeth defeat the Armada of King Philip of Spain, and who, following its defeat, began to build her power and increase her influence abroad. Here were the beginnings of the English, later the British, Empire.

At her death in 1603, Elizabeth (who never married despite numerous offers) left the country secure, and largely free of religious strife. Art and science had flourished during her reign and England was now a first-class power.

clever, vacillating woman – this 'daughter of the devil' as his ambassador had once described her. No longer either, he realized, could his treasury tolerate the piratical activities of a handful of her insolent, heretical subjects – Drake in particular.

The execution of Mary, Queen of Scots, was the final straw. Twixt pious prayers and mountainous piles of correspondence, the Enterprise of England formed in his mind. England, he had decided, from the sanctity of his palace monastery, must be crushed – God willing, of course.

Elizabeth Tudor had inherited, from her father, a navy; but of equal significance, from her grandfather, a shrewdness in money matters. For all the scintillating aura which illumined her forty-five-year-long reign, financial problems consistently dogged this redoubtable Queen. The fight against the Armada was to cost a staggering £160 000 – twice her annual income – and it emptied the nation's war chest. England simply could not afford war. Elizabeth did her utmost to avoid it. Not for her, however, was life an unrelieved round of power, penance and prayer, as with her enemy: she lacked neither dedication nor determination. Yet for admirers and opponents alike, these qualities were mixed with an infuriating dash of feminine disingenuity. Elizabeth of England was born to rule – never to be ruled, by anyone.

It was 1588. Mary had been executed. There had been open conflict in the Netherlands between England and Spain. Philip was infuriated by the predatory activities of the English seaman. There was now no going back. Recoil, as she must, from the immensity of the task ahead – and its cost – Elizabeth realized that the only way to counter an invincible Armada was by means of an invincible England. That was the task. She, and her three and a half million subjects, no longer had any choice in the matter.

The cracks in the fabric of Philip's far-flung empire were, however, becoming evident. It was unmanageable. The possession of England, as Philip must have known, had he paused to reflect, would simply add to his earthly burden. Yet this so-called prudent king pushed on with his Enterprise of England. Ruthlessly, he drew up a plan which was as dogmatic as it was ill-conceived. From the Escorial there issued forth a stream of letters, each with the weighty urgency of royal command, written by a king who had never commanded a ship but who believed, with awesome sincerity, that his guidance was divine.

None dared defy him. From the moment when, in 1587, he issued instructions to his Captain-General of the Oceans, the Marquis of Santa Cruz, to prepare an Armada (the name means simply a fleet of ships), he bullied and cajoled without mercy. Santa Cruz, a great seaman by

The Execution of Mary, Queen of Scots.

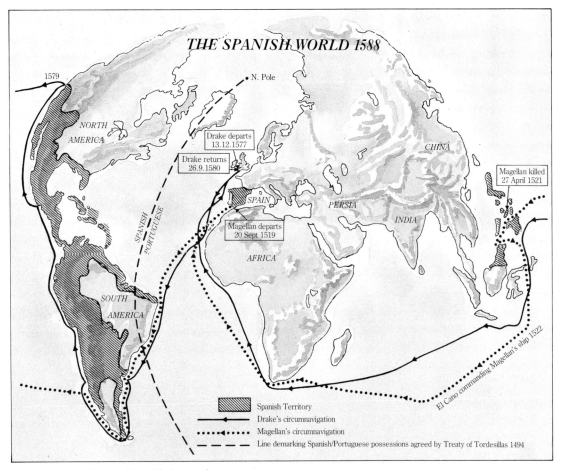

THE SPANISH WORLD 1588

1579

NORTH
AMERICA

N. Pole

Drake departs
13.12.1577

Drake returns
26.9.1580

SPAIN

Magellan departs
20 Sept 1519

CHINA

Magellan killed
27 April 1521

PERSIA

INDIA

AFRICA

SPANISH
PORTUGUESE

SOUTH
AMERICA

El Cano commanding Magellan's ship 1522

Spanish Territory

Drake's circumnavigation

Magellan's circumnavigation

Line demarking Spanish/Portuguese possessions agreed by Treaty of Tordesillas 1494

Spanish possessions in the mid-sixteenth century.

any standard, suffered the indignities with loyal patience – even when Philip announced that if the Armada was not ready to sail in the autumn of 1587 it must depart, prepared or otherwise, in midwinter. He had no idea what problems adverse weather could pose. Santa Cruz died, suddenly, in February 1588, worn out and broken hearted, it is said, at the King's spiteful reproaches and harassment.

On land, the Spanish army had no equal in all Europe and, in the ambitious forty-two-year-old Alexander Farnese, Duke of Parma, it boasted the most successful general of the age. He was Philip's nephew. Yet the King's interminable letters contained no mention of gratitude for Parma's services to his nation in the Netherlands, a contentious and difficult arena of warfare. Increasingly throughout the Armada campaign, Parma's sullen resentment was to become all too obvious. Perhaps he believed that the wily Elizabeth, with whom he was in negotiation (both were playing for time) might, after all, support his vaunting ambition to become King of the Netherlands. Parma, with royal antecedents, believed he had earned the title. Philip needed him to ferry thousands of troops over the narrow sea to South East England, to root out this Protestant heresy by force. The crossing would

be made under the umbrella of the victorious Armada. Parma realized that Philip's plan was, at best, a foolish risk, at worst, a potential catastrophe. Julian of Nassau's powerful fleet of Dutch flyboats – the Sea-Beggars – were daring Parma to venture out across the shallows. Parma realized the futility of such an exercise. His inadequate landing craft would have been smashed to pulp, and troops drowned in their thousands long before they gained the safety of deep water and the shelter of the Armada's guns. Philip, thought Parma, had never listened to advice before, and why should he now? Parma sulked: Nassau waited.

In France, Don Bernardino de Mendoza, ambassador to Philip of Spain, gloated over the discomfort of King Henry III of Valois. Mendoza had been unceremoniously bundled out of England, where he had served as ambassador, for his implication in the Throgmorton plot against Elizabeth. Only his diplomatic status had saved his neck. Impertinently, he had told the Queen's counsellors who saw him off in 1583: 'Tell your mistress that Bernardino de Mendoza was born not to disturb kingdoms, but to conquer them.' In France, it was easy for this arch spymaster to stir up trouble. It was the era of the three Henrys – Valois, Guise and Navarre. The acid-tongued

The Great Hall at Buckland Abbey, with its oak panelling said to have been built to Drake's own design. The intricate carvings reflect the importance of astrological influences. The oak chair (inset) is a replica of one made from the timbers of the Golden Hind, Drake's ship of the circumnavigation.

Valois ruled, but his court of favourites, handsome young men, Mignons, was despised by the rough, turbulent citizenry of Paris. The execution of Mary, Queen of Scots (the king's sister-in-law), gave Mendoza a golden chance to plot with Guise, who was in his pay. Mendoza had old scores to settle, not least revenge upon 'the Englishwoman' – he could not bear to mention Elizabeth by name in the voluminous coded letters sent by courier from Paris to Madrid. On 12 May, 1588, Paris was caught up in the turmoil of the barricades: Henry of Valois was in flight from the mob, Henry of Guise was uncrowned king of the city. Mendoza reported smugly to his royal master in the Escorial that France, at least, would present no threat at all to the passage of the Armada as he, Bernardino de Mendoza, had predicted, promised and arranged.

In Rome, the Pope, Felice Peretti, known as Sixtus V, looked on with remarkable detachment at what was occuring elsewhere in Christendom. Since he was, in theory at least, an integral participant in the plot to overthrow the 'Black Queen', his role on the European chess board was vital. He played his part by pledging one million gold ducats to be paid to Philip when Spanish soldiers should first set foot on English soil. His money was safe.

But 1588 was to prove an even more extra-ordinary year than those prophets of doom, the astrologers, had predicted. To the sixteenth-century mind, magic and the elements went hand in hand. War was a threat. All Europe knew that. To the credulous, something mysterious and terrible threatened, far outweighing temporal fears.

WATER

'The advantage of time and place in all martial actions is half a victory,' scrawled Drake to Queen Elizabeth in April 1588, 'which being lost is irrecoverable.' Nelson, who was to emulate Drake's Cadiz triumph at Trafalgar – so near in place, so far apart in time – was of the same mind: 'Time is everything; five minutes makes the difference between a victory and a defeat.'

Sir Francis Drake, born near that delectable Devonshire town of Tavistock was as unconventional as he was innovative; characteristics which earned him more adulation than abuse. To Philip II he represented the epitome of the sea-devil incarnate, and the King was determined to stamp him out.

When the 'Felicissima Armada' (Fortunate Fleet) was glimpsed over the watery horizon by the English fleet on Saturday 20 July 1588, Drake was there, in his *Revenge*, the greatest mariner of his age in one of its finest vessels, waiting to take full advantage of any false move on the part of the enemy. However, the real excitement had started the previous day, on Friday 19 July, when Captain Thomas Flemyng raced up to Plymouth in his bark, *Golden Hind*. Flemyng had been patrolling the Sleeve, or Chops, the wide expanse of water at the mouth of the English Channel between Ushant and the Scilly Isles. He had seen Spanish ships, sails struck, near the Scillies, evidently waiting for the remainder of the fleet to catch up. Legend has it that Drake was playing bowls on Plymouth Hoe. The Lord Admiral, Charles Howard, might also have been present. Drake was in no hurry. He realized that no ship of any size could sail out of Plymouth Sound against the tide and the south-westerly breeze. The tide was not full until nine o'clock that evening: 'We have time enough to finish the game and beat the Spaniards too,' he observed jovially to Flemyng, as one privateer to another.

For the moment at least, the Armada of Spain, so ponderously heavy, as awesome contemporary reports related, that the sea appeared to groan beneath its weight, had both the advantage of time and place. It was the largest fleet the world had ever witnessed – though Drake (and Santa Cruz) had anticipated it needed at least five-hundred ships to be truly effective. Majestically, it cruised past the coastline of Cornwall, as Philip had ordered. It certainly looked invincible. A crescent-moon formation of one hundred and thirty great ships, like castles afloat. A city upon the sea. For England and Englishmen, this was the moment of truth. All the panicky speculation, all the false alarms, all doubt dramatically removed by this maritime might. Philip of Spain meant business, and here was the spectacular proof positive.

That Friday night, on an ebb tide, the Queen's galleons and armed private merchantmen, warped silently out of the Sound, to anchor beneath the sheltering arm of Rame Head. Around noon, on Saturday, augmented by late

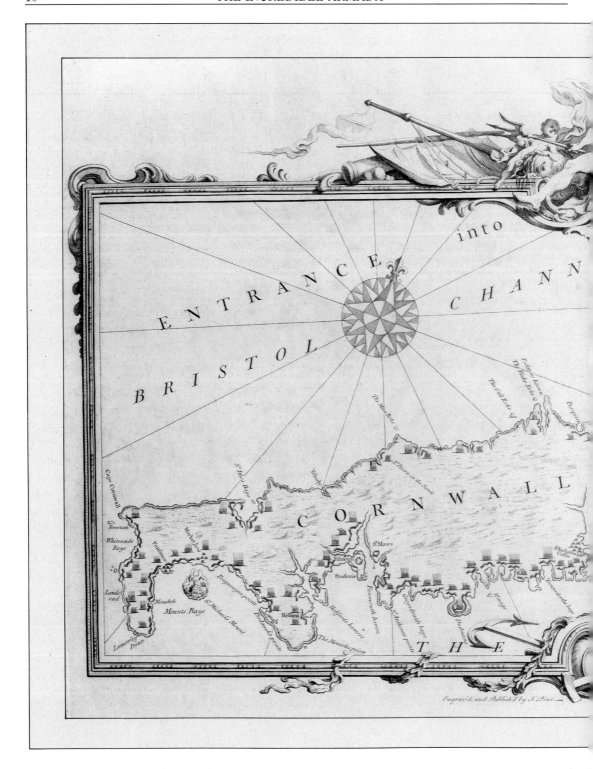

arrivals still straggling out of Plymouth, some fifty-six ships beat a course out towards the Eddystone reefs. Ashore, the people of Plymouth, having worked night and day to service this fleet, strained their eyes for a glimpse of what Flemyng had seen. The town seemed strangely empty after all the activity of the past months.

The seventh Duke of Medina Sidonia, the thirty-seven-year-old Don Alonzo Perez de Guzman el Bueno, captain-general of the Armada, was, by nature, a peaceable man. Family tradition

had it that the Guzmans originated in England, six-hundred years earlier. This senior among Spanish grandees had protested, as vigorously as he dared, at Philip's instruction that he should succeed Santa Cruz as the Armada's commander. The gentle Andalusian hated the sea: 'I know,' he wrote truthfully and miserably to Philip, 'from the small experience I have had afloat, that I am always seasick, and catch cold.' It required honesty and moral courage of a high degree to write such a letter, though three centuries later the jingoistic Victorian writers treated it as

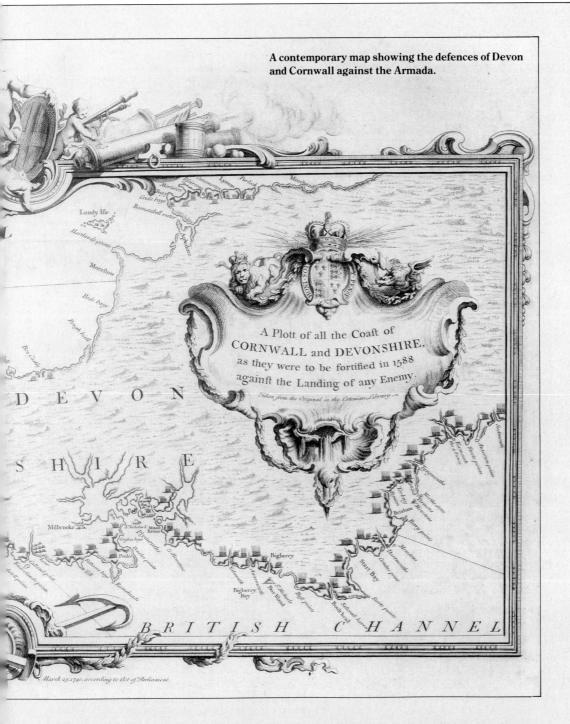

A contemporary map showing the defences of Devon and Cornwall against the Armada.

A Plott of all the Coast of
CORNWALL and DEVONSHIRE,
as they were to be fortified in 1588
against the Landing of any Enemy.

Taken from the Original in the Cottonian Library.

IN DEFENCE OF THE REALM

Like her father, Henry VIII, Elizabeth was ever vigilant against attack and invasion of her island realm. As the threat from the Armada grew, along with the likely invasion of the Duke of Parma's troops from the Continent, Elizabeth appointed Lord Howard of Effingham as admiral in charge of the English navy.

On land, Lord Leicester commanded an amateur army to defend the Essex coast, while in all southern counties militiamen and volunteers formed up under their deputy lieutenants. Sir Richard Grenville and Sir Walter Ralegh laid aside their plans for colonizing the New World and took over the joint defence of Devon and Cornwall.

Plans to counter the invasion were drawn up and arrangements made to issue arms and equipment. Beacons were prepared the length of the land to warn of the invaders, though there is no evidence that they were lit. In the event, land-based troops had little to do other than watch the naval action from various vantage points, or occasionally guard Spanish prisoners brought ashore.

EL DRAQUE

Sir Francis Drake – a portrait by Gheeraerts, held at Buckland Abbey.

Drake's coat of arms – from Buckland Abbey.

'To seek God's enemies and her majesty's where they may be found.'

Recognized as the greatest seaman of his times, Francis Drake was as intent upon serving his Queen as he was his own interests.

Born at Crowndale, near Tavistock, of humble origins, his fame became legendary in his own day, as much feared by the Spanish, his principal foe, as he was revered by his countrymen.

Though not without enemies at Court, and often in disfavour with Elizabeth, he nevertheless remained at the forefront of naval enterprises in England throughout her reign.

In 1577 Drake sailed from Plymouth in command of the 100-ton *Pelican* (later renamed *Golden Hind*) with four other ships on what was to be the first circumnavigation of the globe by an Englishman. It was a remarkable achievement in the face of mutiny, strong Spanish presence, and the uncertainties of weather and disease. He returned to Plymouth in September 1580 in a ship laden with treasure and spices worth an estimated half-million pounds. For this achievement he was knighted by the Queen. With his share of the plunder from the voyage, Drake bought Buckland Abbey, former home of the Grenvilles.

Drake took part in many later expeditions during which he became the scourge of Spanish ships returning with treasure from the Indies. His attack upon Cadiz was typical of his daring seamanship and bravado.

Short, stocky and red-haired, he was essentially a man of action. He may have been ruthless, ambitious and boastful, but he was also generous, cheerful and an ideal leader of men.

JOHN HAWKYNS

Sir John Hawkyns (1532-95) by Custodis, now in Buckland Abbey.

'Serve God daily, love one another, preserve your victuals, beware of fire, and keep good company.'

Sir John Hawkyns (or Hawkins) was born in Plymouth, the son of a hardhitting, coarse-tongued merchant, William senior, a mayor of Plymouth who, like Drake, was raised near Tavistock.

John's character was the very opposite of his father's; genial, charming, alert and well-dressed, he entertained King Philip II of Spain in Plymouth in 1557, having met him as a prince in 1555 on his first visit to England.

The Hawkyns family had long traded with West Africa, but John became the first English slave trader, antagonizing the Portuguese whose trade he was adopting. In recognition of his trading origins John's crest depicted a demi-Moor proper, bound. Elizabethans had no scruples in such matters.

His career and marriage (to the daughter of Benjamin Gonson, treasurer to the navy), took him to London, but John remained true to Plymouth. He was a man ahead of his times, considerate for his men's welfare – a concern he shared with his distant cousin, Drake, though Hawkyns appeared more caring and cautious about overcrowding in his ships. The two great mariners enjoyed a mutual hatred of the Spanish as a result of treachery in 1569 at San Juan de Ulua (now Vera Cruz). Neither could forget it. Drake might even have recalled the event with some sense of embarrassment.

The Hawkyns family did more than any other to advance the cause of Plymouth in the sixteenth century, making it an ocean port, a naval base, a refuge for privateers, and the western bastion of England's defences. No single man did more, however, than John Hawkyns in perfecting Elizabeth's splendid new navy of which he became treasurer in 1577. In this position, despite the nagging parsimony of his masters, he fashioned a superb fleet of twenty-five fighting ships of over a hundred tons, and eighteen sea-going pinnaces. He was responsible for increasing the pay of the Queen's sailors by a third – to ten shillings per month – and afforded the rise by reducing the size of the crews, and thereby the diseases to which they were prone.

Hawkyns oversaw the imaginative restyling of the English galleons, which were no longer ungainly carrack-built floating castles, such as he had once handled, but sleek, streamlined, trim and nimble men o'war, which ran rings around the Armada's cumbersome bulk (yet it must be remembered, Frobisher's old *Triumph*, at around 1200 tons, was the largest vessel on either side). Such were Hawkyns's ships, so stout and true that they seemed to have been carved from solid oak.

On 26 July, 1588, John Hawkyns was finally knighted, in battle, aboard Howard's flagship, the *Ark Royal*. Ten years of battle against lies and corruption, noted his biographer, J. A. Williamson, were justified in ten days of fighting against the Armada.

signifying cowardice. Seasick or not, Medina Sidonia nobly rose to the occasion despite his lack of experience and gravely expressed reservations about his competence for such a command.

As the Lizard loomed into sight at four o'clock on the afternoon of Friday, 19 July, he may well have permitted himself a sigh of relief. The royal standard was hoisted to the fore of the flagship, the *San Martin*, and at the main, a sacred flag depicting the crucifix between the figures of the Virgin and St Mary Magdalene. Somewhere ahead, Medina Sidonia realized, lay the English fleet, still in harbour, perhaps, their hulls painted geometrically in the Queen's colours of green and white. Behind him lay a nightmarish voyage of violent storms, occupying fifty troublesome days since the Armada cleared Lisbon and re-grouped at Corunna. Perhaps he reflected on his graceful home and family at San Lucar, but never far from his uppermost thoughts were his royal master's instructions: 'In the first place, as all victories are the gift of God Almighty, and the course we champion is so exceedingly His, we may fairly look for His aid and favour, unless by our sins we render ourselves unworthy.'

No blasphemy on board – no harlots since, apart from other considerations, preached the moralists of the time, sexual indulgence opened the pores to infection. To the hellish discomfort of the decks, crowded with soldiers and sailors, was added below the nauseous smell of vomit, excreta and bloody flux – or dysentery. Wooden cesspits!

The Armada was the largest fleet of its kind ever to put to sea for a long voyage. Over 19000 soldiers were crammed into these ships, along with more than 8000 sailors, 2000 galley slaves, 1400 volunteers, and around 180 monks and friars. There was also a not inconsiderable number of animals, especially mules and horses, of whose fate we shall learn later.

Perhaps this Spanish grandee might also have been reminded, as the landscape of Cornwall with its sturdy church towers came into view, of the colossal religious service at Lisbon in April, when the Armada standard was ritually blessed by the papal representative. The polyglot force, drawn from all quarters of the many Latin countries, had confessed their sins and made peace with their maker. Friars had read aloud the papal absolution, and listed the indulgences granted to those labouring on this epic mission. '*Exurge, Domine, et vindica causam tuam* – Arise, O Lord, and

Even before the Armada sailed into the Channel, the orders given to its commander were known to the English. This is the title page of a book published in London even as Medina Sidonia's ships neared the English coast. The book included details of rendezvous points, rations, and rules of behaviour among the Spanish sailors.

The battle off Plymouth.

vindicate thy cause.' Such words lived on in the mind. This, the Duke may well have thought as he shivered in the cool westerly breeze of this northern clime, was, after all, a Holy Crusade. Such thoughts were comforting and reassuring. But where, wondered Medina Sidonia, was the English fleet? He was soon to know.

Saturday's dawn brought in a thick drizzle – but the sea was calm. The wind, however, was restless, and soon began to freshen up from the west. It was weather with which all Westcountrymen are long familiar. While the Armada continued its slow and stately progress eastwards, in close formation, past Falmouth, a Spanish pinnace, under Ensign Juan Gil, returned from reconnoitre with the four-man crew of a captured Falmouth fishing boat. Howard and Drake, they told their captors, had sailed from Plymouth with the fleet.

The King's captain-general convened his first council of war on the strength of what the fishermen had told him. The Armada was now between ten and twelve leagues from Plymouth – some thirty to thirty-six nautical miles. From subsequent reports it is clear they discussed the possibility of entering and attacking the port. The idea of a decisive early battle and gaining a foothold on the mainland, appealing a prospect as it seemed to at least one military adviser on board, was rejected.

Medina Sidonia's instructions were clear. He was to link up with Parma's seaborne troops at Dunkirk, guiding them across to South East England as an invasion force. But where was the rendezvous to be? 'Off the Isle of Wight' suggested the Duke in his despatch sent back to the King by speedy pinnace after the council meeting: 'The plan is that at the moment of my arrival he [the Duke of Parma] should sally forth with the fleet not causing me to wait a minute.' Misguided man. How appalled Medina Sidonia would have been had he been able to witness Parma's state of unreadiness, and the flimsiness of his flotilla. Moreover, Medina Sidonia was unaware that at three o'clock that Saturday afternoon, as the shrouding mist lifted off the sea, his Armada had been seen by the English fleet, now manoeuvring itself into position, to lie in wait for the enemy. The Armada sailed on, in comfortably tight formation, gracefully, unknowingly, straight into the trap.

Early on the morning of Sunday, 21 July, the moonlight broke through the mist, casting its pale gleam over the ocean. The sea seemed deserted to the Spanish. Vacant. Innocuous. Even as day broke, to their surprise and consternation they still appeared to be alone. But the sudden shrill scream of a cannonball pulled their attention landwards, and to a handful of Plymouth ships, including Martin Frobisher's high-charged galleon, the *Triumph*. Contemptuously, though

hugely outnumbered, the English let fly at Recalde's Biscayan Squadron. In an instant, the surprised Spaniards realized that these English ships were as fast as greyhounds. But a much greater shock followed hard on the heels of the first. In a swirl of sail, the main English fleet appeared on the horizon, advancing at what seemed an electrifying speed to windward at the Armada's rear. Like a pack of angry terriers over fifty English ships swept down upon the Armada, snapping and barking with their cannonfire at the bull's great flanks. Lord Howard's own pinnace *Disdain* led the pack, skimming effortlessly over the waves to deliver her Admiral's challenge, cocking defiance at the great castellated galleons of Spain. The English fleet followed, racing past, insolently close in dramatic single-line formation. The wooden monsters groaned and shuddered as the wave of fire struck. The Armada's right wing bulged precariously out of its half-moon formation. The Duke's presence of mind saved

Above: English galleons attack a galleass and dismast a stricken carrack, while the tightly-packed Spanish fleet fills the seas behind.

Right: An engraving – one of a series commissioned by Lord Howard, Admiral of the English fleet – charting the progress of the Armada. Here is shown the perfect crescent of the Spanish fleet as it nears Plymouth. Also shown is the course of the English fleet out of Plymouth, and its disposition at the rear of the Armada.

the situation. As panic began to infiltrate the fleet, he steered his flagship protectively towards the action, to face up to this enemy who, by some devil's trick, had gained the initiative.

The Armada closed its mighty ranks. But the Duke was greatly worried. Never before had he, or his seamen, witnessed such stinging tactics on

King ♣

The English Fleet whereof the L.d Charles How.ard was L.d Admi.rall & S.r Fran: Drake vice Admirall.

Lord Howard of Effingham, Admiral of the English fleet, gave Drake, Frobisher and Hawkyns each command of a squadron. This is depicted in a series of playing cards produced in England to celebrate the Armada victory.

Queen ♦

The 2.d Squadron ruled by S.r Francis Drake

water. He learned, that day, a singular truth, that battle by boarding was the strategy of another age – the past. Battle by bombardment was the ploy of the future. It was, in the annals of naval warfare, a day of historic importance. Despairingly, Medina Sidonia and his squadron commanders watched the departing English – too fast by far to pursue – and realized at that moment that the Armada, splendid seaborne fortress though it was, was not designed to cope with such tactics. The days ahead were to compound that knowledge and reinforce their sense of dejection. Howard's fleet, its brief but telling encounter complete, curved away to a safe distance, to reform and watch and wait with the advantages of a favourable wind. Spain's captain-general had more urgent matters to deal with. As the Spanish fleet compacted into tight formation, Don Pedro de Valdes' vessel, the *Rosario*, was crippled in a collision with a sister ship. The second problem was more serious. A sudden explosion rent the air from the far wing of the Armada. Oquendo's vice-flagship, the *San Salvador*, burst into flames from an explosion among the barrels of gunpowder on her quarter deck. Men lay burnt and dying on her decks. Two hundred were killed by the explosion. Howard and Drake took note.

Ashore on that Sunday morning, the towns-people of Plymouth viewed the engagement at sea from their several safe vantage points. The ancients among them may have wondered why there had been no grappling with the enemy: why Howard, the Lord Admiral, appeared to have called off the action so early in the proceedings. It was still only one o'clock. The observers expected the English to renew their attack, and to press home their advantage. Some might have seen from the shore a ball of fire as the *San Salvador* blew up. Whose was that, they must have wondered – ours or theirs? But Howard was right. The Spanish military superiority was overwhelming. It would have been suicide to attempt to board any vessel behind that great defensive sea wall: 'We durst not advantage to put in among them, their fleet being so strong,' he wrote.

Drake scrawled, in low key, 'There have passed some cannon shot – they are determined to sell their lives with blows.' The Mayor of

Plymouth, William Hawkyns, wrote excitedly to the Privy Council. 'The Spanish fleet was in view of this town yesternight, and my Lord Admiral was passed to the sea before our said view, and was ought of our sight. Since which time we have certain knowledge, as also by plain views this present morning [Sunday] that my lord being to the windwards of the enemy, are in fight, which we beheld.' But if good Mayor William had cause for excitement, his brother John, commanding the *Victory* against the Armada, could have been forgiven for blushing with pride.

Howard knew how foolhardy it would have been to press home the Sunday morning engagement off Plymouth. Reinforcements lay ahead, and he already needed more ammunition. But Howard would also have been wondering if, and where, the Armada might attempt to land an invading party. Torbay? Portland? The Isle of

The 3ᵈ Squadron ruled by Hawkins.

Wight? His council of war that Sunday afternoon aboard the *Ark Royal* might well have conceived a plan to contain the enemy fleet and prevent a landing by harassment on three sides: to shepherd it towards Dover into the jaws of the second English fleet waiting there. We may only speculate on English strategy. There is no record of those deliberations. Yet a discernible pattern began to emerge.

Medina Sidonia had problems enough. The

Rosario, flagship of the Andalusian contingent, was now wallowing helplessly in the freshening breeze: the *San Salvador*, vice flagship of the Guipozcoan armada, still smouldered from the explosion. In addition, Recalde's Biscayan flagship, the *San Juan*, severely battered by *Revenge*, *Victory* and *Triumph*, needed urgent repairs. The Duke decided to take the *San Salvador* in tow – it was the best he could do. But soon, the entire fleet, stretched out some four miles or more from end to end, heard distress signals boom out. It was Don Pedro de Valdes in the *Rosario*. Frantically, they tried to take her in tow. The sea was rising, fast. The tow snapped. Diego Flores de Valdes, the Duke's adviser, was consulted. Abandon her, he coolly recommended. Do not jeopardize the safety of the remainder by hanging about, he warned the Duke. The Armada sailed on, leaving Don Pedro to his fate. The dull rumble of distant gunfire astern as night enfolded the Spanish battle fleet enraged soldiers and sailors alike. Were not Don Pedro and Diego Flores kinsmen, they asked themselves? Yes, and deadly enemies also. The whole fleet knew it. Morale sank. They blamed Diego and never forgave him.

Howard had bestowed upon Drake, his second-in-command, the honour of leading the English fleet in pursuit of the enemy that gloomy Sunday evening. But early on Monday morning, 22 July,

The 4ᵗʰ Squadron ruled by Forbisher.

the stern light on Drake's *Revenge*, a beacon the fleet was so assiduously following, was suddenly extinguished without warning. Drake explained later that he left the watch to pursue certain hulks, believing them to be part of a possible Spanish manoeuvre to outwit the English. By a most extraordinary coincidence (though some entertained darker thoughts about Drake's ulterior motives) the great seadog, whose sense of direction was invariably faultless wherever treasure was concerned, turned up alongside the crippled *Rosario*. Don Pedro surrendered, with no nonsense – who could refuse El Draque? Prisoners were taken as well as valuable munitions and 50 000 escudos, which Drake promptly impounded aboard the *Revenge* to await

the Queen's pleasure. The *Rosario* was despatched, under tow, to Torbay, and Don Pedro was given an honoured place in Drake's cabin, from where he was to enjoy a grandstand view of the battle ahead.

Such nice courtesy merely served to incense Drake's critics. The bluff Yorkshireman, Martin Frobisher, was livid when he learned what Drake had been up to. He would have his share of the spoils, he declared, or 'the best blood in his [Drake's] belly.' Drake, he declared, was both a coward and a cozening cheat. Drake, however, was impervious to such slander. The age in which he lived set great store by the simple virtue of achievement – the ends justified the means. The establishment may have regarded this brave,

The Surrender, by Seymour Lucas, now at Buckland Abbey. Admiral Don Pedro de Valdes, aboard the *Revenge*, hands his sword to Drake following the capitulation of the *Nuestra Senora del Rosario.*

ambitious and very lucky Devon man as an upstart, but to the Elizabethans at large Drake could do no wrong. The *Rosario* was stripped of her cannon and munitions, and the local populace then took its share, so that by the time the deputy lieutenants arrived to take the prize there was little worth having. Later, she was taken to Dartmouth where, it is said, some of her timbers were used to construct the church gallery. In 1589 she was taken to Chatham.

Howard had been close behind Drake. Puzzled by the disappearance of the leading light, he sped on, in the darkness, in company with two other English ships the *Mary* and the *White Bear* only to discover, at first light off Berry Head, Torbay, that he was almost within range of the Armada's

rear guns. Howard, doubtless, was shocked and, had Medina Sidonia been alert to his adversary's plight, and quickly closed the 'horns' of the crescent tight about the trio of English ships, the Lord Admiral of England might well have been trapped, and crushed. But Howard's predicament passed unnoticed, and he slipped away to rejoin the fleet then so far distant that it was scarcely visible on the horizon.

Howard accepted Drake's explanation of his detour without comment, but it is significant that Drake received no mention in Howard's *Relation of the Proceedings* thereafter. Later that day, the English picked up the sinking *San Salvador*, and Thomas Flemyng was detached in the *Golden Hind* to tow it into Weymouth. The stench of

The *Revenge* engages the Spanish rearguard.

burnt flesh nauseated the boarding party but the stricken ship yielded up valuable supplies of munitions.

Early on Tuesday morning, 23 July, the wind veered east over Lyme Bay. A sea fight had begun off Portland; 'sharp and long' it was, reported John Hawkyns. The Armada, with an easterly in its sails, swung around to face its pursuers and, for a time, the English looked disorganized. Ships attached themselves to the leaders whom they knew, and trusted. Two days later, Howard, conscious of this defect, was to reorganize battle formation into four squadrons under himself, Drake, Frobisher and Hawkyns.

Apart from a skirmish at dawn, Wednesday passed almost without incident. The gloom lifted, and the sun shone. The Armada lumbered on, at an average speed of two knots, making painfully slow progress yet preserving its crescent, or half-moon formation, a tribute to the skill and discipline shown by the Spanish navigators. During the night, the fleets passed St Alban's Head. At dawn, on Thursday 25 July, Medina Sidonia saw white cliffs ahead. It was the Isle of Wight. Surely the time for a great decision was now. Yet despite the repeated letters which he had sent ahead to Parma there had been no word in reply. The silence bewildered him. As the Armada began to approach the entrance to the Solent, the obedient Duke paused to reflect again. He was running short of ammunition. Dare he risk an attack upon Wight to establish a beach-head with the infantry and find a safe, anchorage for the fleet to await Parma's arrival?

The King's instructions on this point had been: 'On no account will you enter the Isle of Wight on your way up, nor before you have made every possible effort to carry out the main idea.' That was plain enough.

The English fleet, happily augmented by more ships and ammunition, stood ready to pounce – on three sides. But the lack of wind proved as much an embarrassment to Howard as it did to the Duke. Frobisher, in the *Triumph*, blocked any precipitate move on the Armada's part to disembark soldiers – had such an idea been entertained. But as on the Tuesday, in the tidal race off Portland, the old, high-sided galleon ran into an awkward position. It has been suggested that Frobisher was playing the part of a decoy, but it took eleven longboats to tow him clear.

Drake and Hawkyns, darting hither and thither, tried to push the Armada towards the sharp Owers reefs, north of the approaches to Spithead. Howard's squadron won its spurs in the thick of the five-hour long fight. But it was as indecisive as before. From the smoke of battle, the great half moon emerged, still in formation, but committed now, finally and irrevocably, for the straits of Dover. Ahead, longing to join battle, were the squadrons of Seymour and Wynter. Astern, still snapping and snarling in the Armada's wake, were four English squadrons gaining in confidence with each passing hour.

'I expect,' wrote the Duke to Parma, 'to be on the Flemish coast very soon.' He inquired again for ships with powder and ball. Parma, however, remained silent and unseen.

LEO

FIRE

The possibility of employing fireships to scatter the mighty Armada was already engaging English minds. This enemy fleet was tougher than they had anticipated; its discipline was exemplary; the wooden wall looked impenetrable – a very formidable war machine, with towers and turrets bristling with guns advancing deliberately, if slowly, up Channel. It seemed unstoppable. The English fleet was short of shot and powder after the battle off Wight – yet they celebrated as if it had been an unqualified triumph. In the stillness of Friday morning Howard knighted Hawkyns and Frobisher aboard the *Ark Royal*, the highest decoration he was permitted to confer. Of the two fleets, after a sorely trying and tormenting week in the surging Channel, the English looked in much better shape. Yet for all the expenditure of shot, all the deafening, thunderous roar of British cannon and culverin, and the blustering response from the best weaponry the King of Spain could muster, the battle by bombardment was still proving indecisive. The Spanish fumed. This was not the warfare they had prepared for. They had come ready to fight in hand-to-hand combat. The British tactics rudely shocked them. The English intention, 'so to course the enemy as they shall have no leisure to land', was a success, though Howard may have been grieved that the Armada's long range weapons seemed as powerful as his own. After Wight, he realized that if they were to sink these Spanish castles, the battle must be fought from closer quarters. Drake knew that too, but battle by boarding was ruled out. How to disperse them though? Fire?

The previous year, Sir Francis Drake, in a typically intrepid action, danced past the defences of Cadiz and created chaos among the gathering Armada. With banners fluttering and trumpets braying and kettle-drums sounding defiance, he plunged down upon an unsuspecting medley of shipping resting quietly at anchor and created mayhem. This brilliant, spectacular and daring piece of opportunism, however much it earned him the emnity of his second-in-command, William Borough, added to the legendary aura. The English corsair had thus 'singed the King of Spain's beard'. All Europe laughed at the exploit. But in real terms, it had put paid to Philip's plans for a 1587 invasion, giving the Queen, country and navy, valuable breathing space.

On Saturday, 27 July, the Armada crossed the Channel from Sussex to the French coast. The English were in close pursuit. From Hastings to Rye, the fishermen of the Cinque ports had been asked to send boats to Dover Castle, where brushwood and plentiful supplies of pitch were heaped on board. The Queen's man, Richard Barry, was preparing nineteen fireships.

At sea, off Cap Gris Nez, with the wind blowing from the south-west, and amid intermittent showers of rain, the Armada suddenly dropped anchor, the entire fleet coming to an abrupt halt. It was a dramatic and deliberate piece of

HELL BURNERS – THE FIRESHIPS

Ever since the Byzantines created Greek Fire by pumping an inflammable liquid through tubes set in the bows of their warships, men had been perfecting fire as an instrument of naval warfare. The Spanish had good cause to fear the use of fire against the Armada, Philip had warned Medina Sidonia – by letter, of course – that the English would employ 'offensive fireworks'. Both the King and the Duke, and probably many of those sailing in the cramped wooden hulls of the crowded Armada, would be recalling the Italian inventor, Federigo Giambelli, who three years earlier had been responsible for almost a thousand Spanish deaths in a single explosion on the Scheldt estuary, when the Duke of Parma himself had been lucky to escape with his life. Philip now knew that Giambelli was in England working for Elizabeth.

Giambelli's device was known as the *máquina de mina* (the mine machine), or more popularly as the 'Antwerp hell-burner'. He had created this weapon by lining the hull of a ship with bricks, loading it with barrels of gunpowder, covering these with rocks and scraps of iron, and setting a time mechanism of clock-operated flintlocks. After a set interval, the time-bomb exploded, showering a deadly hail of broken stone and shrapnel far and wide. Giambelli's wicked device had taken the Spanish at Antwerp completely by surprise. An innocent-looking ship fetched up beside the fortified bridge around which unsuspecting guards had crowded, suddenly blew up spewing destruction over a half-mile radius.

However, the fireships sent in against the Armada were not mine machines but ordinary sailing craft soaked in tar, cannons primed to explode as they approached the panic-striken Spanish fleet. While the battle raged, Giambelli was in London designing an unnecessary protective boom across the Thames. It has been said – and certainly many Spanish schoolchildren are taught – that Philip's private secretary, Antonio Perez, was a double agent, spying for both sides. If that was so, Philip appears to have been poorly informed.

Left: The English watch and wait as fireships move in towards the massed Spanish fleet. Already there is panic amongst the Spanish crews.

Below: Giambelli's 'Hell Burners' at Antwerp.

DEROUTE DU PONT FARNESE

LIVING HISTORY – THE THOMAS

The lading accounts of materials from militia stores taken on board Drake's ship *Thomas* – the crosses (numerals) against each item denoting a quantity of ten, twenty, etc. Shown as being taken on board at Plymouth before the Armada sailed are:

Powder . . . seven barrels: Roundshot for Sacre . . . 35: For Minion . . . 50: For Fawcon . . . 15: Stone shot for fowlers . . .15: Muskette complete . . . 15: Callivers furnished . . . 30: Match . . . 150 pounds: Bows . . . 15: Arrows . . . 30: sheaves: Long Pikes . . . 25: Short Pikes . . . 15: Black bills . . . 25.

The moment it was decided to send in fireships against the Armada, it must have been obvious to the English commanders that their plan to fetch suitable ships from Dover would take too long to implement. Impatient to make the most of favourable tide and winds, and with the great Armada at anchor before them, the English selected ships from those present to act as fireships. These were: Captain Yonge's flyboat *Bear*, of 140 tons (valued at £550); Cure's ship of 150 tons (£600); the 130 ton *Angel* of Hampton (£450); the 200-ton *Thomas* of Plymouth, owned by Sir Francis Drake (£1000); the barque *Talbot*, a 200-ton Westcountry ship (£900); the 150-ton barque *Bond*, owned by Sir John Hawkyns (£600); the *Hope*, 180 tons (of Plymouth), owned by William Hart (£600); and the 90-ton *Elizabeth* of Lowestoft, owned by Thomas Meldrum (£416). Seldom, if ever, has £5000 been better spent in the service of England.

seamanship which might have caught less watchful pursuers unaware. The English too were forced to anchor otherwise they would have swept past the Armada and lost wind advantage. Some four miles from Calais, with the two fleets anchored, the Duke received his worst news to date. The pilots warned him that they could not, dared not, take him into Dunkirk. They were correct. Not one, let alone over a hundred troopships had sufficiently shallow draughts safely to negotiate the single, narrow channel which cut through the massive sandbanks along this coastline. Dunkirk was little more than a sandy creek. One more mistake had been added to the growing catalogue of errors. Incredibly, until this moment, no one appeared to have taken this simple fact into consideration, least of all the vague architect of this grandiose plan, Philip of Spain. The two fleets remained poised, scarcely a culverin-shot apart.

The little English force of just over fifty which had warped out of Plymouth Sound a week ago, and which had now fought three great sea battles, had grown to a force of around one hundred and forty. Many were small, privately owned ships: volunteers, in fact, and reminiscent of that courageous fleet of small boats which was to assemble, three and a half centuries later, to rescue the British army from the hands of the Germans at Dunkirk.

COMPENSATION–
AN ERROR IN ACCOUNTING

The page taken from Drake's accounts book held at Buckland Abbey which shows the compensation claim for the cost of his involvement in the Armada.

Burghley, ever on the lookout for peculation, audited Drake's expenses for Armada Year, and disputed the claim of '1000 for the loss at Calais of the Thomas' – one of the fireships.

State papers reveal that Drake was compensated for the sacrifice of his ship in October 1588, and this duplication may have been simply an error by Drake's secretary in whose neat handwriting the claim was submitted. Burghley's annotations appear in the margin.

That Drake was a man of great wealth can be gauged from the large sums he disbursed in victualling his own and other crews. Evidently, Captain Thomas Fenner and others received no reimbursement of their expenses until the Lord Admiral (Howard) arrived in Plymouth.

Drake's claim for powder and other supplies is also revealing: 100 barrels of corn powder at £5 each, 50 longbows (£8. 6s. 3d) and 100 sheaves of arrows (£10). In all, he claimed £4751 on this occasion (reduced by £1000 by Burghley, who did note that, however, there was 'more to be allowed unto Sir F Drake for Emptions and sundry charges').

Included in that total are expenses for carpenters, drummers, pursers, boatswains, surgeons, cooks, musicians, travel to Court, £100 given in reward to the company of the Revenge 'after the second dayes fight' and £150 for the cost of 'apparell for Don Pedro and the rest of the Spaniards with him'.

This is perhaps the most gorgeous of all contemporary Armada pictures. The scene, in oil on wood, shows the two fleets engaged in battle. The Spanish ships display scarlet flags emblazoned with gold, the English show the flag of St George, white with a red cross. The ship in the right foreground possibly represents Howard's flagship, the *Ark Royal*.

On Sunday, as the fleets rode at anchor, Medina Sidonia confided to his war diary: 'The enemy's fleet was re-inforced by 36 sail, including five great galleons.' The signs were ominous. To other Spanish observers, the English appeared as 'a great presentiment of evil from that devilish people and their arts.'* The Duke sent his emissaries ashore, to advise the Governor of Calais why he had anchored in French waters. They found his excellency the Governor, and his lady, seated in a coach, near the beach, waiting for the battle to begin! The Governor politely sent a basket of fruit to the Duke, and a warning on the hazards of the coastline – but no ammunition. Calais intended to adopt a neutral stance in any struggle between the arrogant Spanish and the mad Englishmen. At long last, however, the Duke received a letter from Parma. His blood ran cold. The news confounded him. Parma, at Bruges, not Dunkirk, explained it would take a fortnight at least to prepare the invasion army for England. Parma also wrote that day to his uncle, the King: 'Most of our boats are only built for rivers, and they are unable to weather the least sea.' Parma, confronted with the arrival of a fleet he had never expected to see (and never would, in fact), was as unready as he was unwilling to come out and face either the Dutch or the English.

All day long men from the Spanish fleet passed from ship to shore, filling water casks, buying food. Howard looked on, fearing the worst – that the French were providing military assistance. But Medina Sidonia, regaining his composure after Parma's letter, was worried also. What were those English devils up to?

Howard hung out his flag for early morning council. Wynter, the veteran seaman, whose gallant action thirty years before had saved Scotland from the French, and who had now joined the fleet along with Seymour's squadron, wrote after the assembly that 'it had been concluded that the practice for the "firing of ships" should be put into execution the night following [i.e. Monday] and Sir Henry Palmer was assigned to bear over presently [immediately] in a pinnace for Dover, to bring away such vessels as were fit to be fired and materials after to take fire.' The wind was fresh, gusting uncomfortably from the west. Sir Henry, the English soon realized, could hardly be expected to return in

* Howarth – The Voyage of the Armada – p.170

time for an attack the following night. They moved with alacrity, and that was what so disturbed the observant Medina Sidonia. The tide was running from the west – towards his fleet. The English had made up their minds, and Drake and Hawkyns would have been chuckling through their beards. Improvised fireships would be sent in, at midnight.

From the compensation claims later submitted by ship owners to the Treasury, for cod, beef and butter, cheese, candles, beer and biscuits, we know which vessels were sacrificed in that fiery fleet, and may better appreciate the haste of preparation.

Hawkyns would have remembered, as his men stacked the barque *Bond* with combustibles, how he had panicked at San Juan de Ulua when the Spanish launched their fireships at his vessel, the

Jesus: Drake, always ready to haul with his men, might have thought of the ships he had fired, the previous April, in Cadiz. As night closed in, preparations were completed. The ordnance aboard the eight vessels chosen as fireships were left loaded, so that as they came down upon the neap tide in the dark their approach would be heralded in the most fearsome way imaginable – by shattering explosions. Their skeleton crews waited nervously on board listening anxiously for the single gunshot which would be the signal for attack. The silence must have been profound.

On that Sunday afternoon in July, off Calais, Medina Sidonia guessed correctly what his opponents were planning to do, and he must have shuddered at the possibility that they were preparing more of the diabolical Giambelli hell-burners. He ordered out a screen of longboats

and pinnaces equipped with grappling irons to haul the English fireships clear of his fleet, and issued instructions to commanders that on no account were they to abandon their moorings. As the clouds scudded across the face of a quarter-moon, the Armada crews waited, with terror in their hearts. At the second watch – midnight – the English unleashed their inferno.

It sputtered slowly into life, glowing eerily as first two, then all eight ships lit up the night waters. The wind, and the current of some three and a half knots, carried them straight towards the floating city – the walls of wood. Now abandoned by their crews, and with lines of fire flickering up and down their rigging engulfing the canvas of their set sails, they swept in uncannily perfect formation for over a mile towards the Armada. It was an unearthly spectacle and, not surprisingly, the Spanish, fearful that these monsters might explode and shower a deadly salvo of missiles into their midst, panicked. The crewmen in the screen made a brave, and partially successful initial attempt to grapple with this fiery horror. But at that moment, the cannons, primed and loaded, and now overheated, thundered into life, scattering shot far and wide. As fountains of sparks shot skywards, discipline disintegrated. With thoughts of Giambelli in their minds, and *maquinas de minas* on their lips, Spanish crews abandoned control and slashed through anchor cables. The great ships scattered into the night, while the fireships pulsated onwards through a gaping black hole, beaching themselves on the French coast, and burning out harmlessly like spent fireworks.

The Duke, whose flagship had re-anchored with four other royal galleons of Spain not a mile from the incident, endeavoured to rally his forces. But the English grand fleet was now ready to deliver the *coup de grace*.

Then, to the bewilderment of all expectations gained from that incident on the night of 28-29 July, the Lord Admiral, Charles Howard, made an error of judgment. No doubt he was being hard pressed from Westminster to take prizes of war to defray costs, but his single mistake in what, otherwise, was an outstanding command, cost his fleet what many historians believe would have been outright victory. Having agreed that he would lead the assault of the English squadrons upon the scattered Armada, his *Ark Royal* veered away in pursuit of a Spanish galleass, the *San Lorenzo* which, rudder broken, lay stricken and helpless on the sandbanks beneath the walls of Calais castle. While Howard dithered and wasted precious time trying to extricate a prize of war, it fell to Sir Francis Drake, the second-in-command, to lead what was to be, in fact, the fourth, and final English assault on the Spanish Armada. On that Monday morning off the little port of Gravelines, the sea was rough, the wind strong, freshening from the north-west. No great sea battle had ever been fought under such conditions. But this time, under Drake's leadership, the English were determined to make every shot tell.

'How much nearer, so much the better,' wrote Richard Hawkyns of the *Swallow*. This son of the splendid architect of the British Navy, was blooded in battle that day. Gravelines, our history books and teachers tell us, was one of the decisive battles in world history. Medina Sidonia had managed to reassemble his ragged, struggling fleet. He was wise enough to realize that his defiance was but a prelude to certain defeat, but noble enough to fight on, gallantly.

Drake drove the great *Revenge* towards the San Martin, holding his fire until the two ships were scarcely half a musket shot apart, some hundred paces. The English man o'war was pierced through repeatedly by the guns of the *San Martin*, but on she came and, from close range, hurled a massive bellyful of fury into the Spanish flagship. Fenner, following in the *Nonpareil*, sped after the great admiral, following his example, and one after another the remainder of Drake's squadron unleashed themselves upon the hapless Spanish. Drake, with his uncanny instinct, led the way north, in search of other prey. He realized that the ships of Spain were struggling desperately to reform and to steer clear of the wicked, shallow banks of sand, and certain death by foundering on a foreign coastline. Across the centuries though we hear the complaint of Drake's actions by Frobisher: 'Bragging up at the first indeed ... then kept his

SHIPS OF THE ENGLISH FLEET

Throughout almost the whole passage of the Armada up the English Channel, the English fleet had the advantage of the wind, and certainly the Spanish tactics played into the hands of the English captains. The tight, crescent-shaped formation allowed the English ships to move in against the enemy when the wind allowed, then to escape before the Spanish ships could join battle. Though the Spanish ships were at least as well-armed as their adversaries and were captained by fine seamen, they were never allowed the advantage of close-quarter fighting in which their troop-carrying ships would have been most dangerous. The hit-and-run strategy employed by the English was perfectly suited to the speed and manoeuvreability of their vessels which also had the advantage of being resupplied from the shore as munitions ran low.

Ark Royal
Completed in 1587, the 800-ton *Ark Royal* was one of the newest additions to the English fleet. Built to Sir Walter Raleigh's orders and donated to the fleet in return for a £5000 I.O.U., she carried four masts, and a complement of 270 seamen.

She became the flagship of Lord Howard who wrote of her: 'I think her the one ship in the world for all conditions.'

White Bear
One of the largest of the English fleet at 1000 tons, *White Bear* had a crew of 500 seamen and was heavily gunned. Throughout the battle against the Armada she appears to have sailed close to Lord

luff, and was glad he was gone again like a cowardly knave or traitor.' He might better have reserved his criticism for Howard, who finally brought the *Ark Royal* out of the scrappy, time-consuming skirmish off Calais to rejoin the fleet which he ought to have been leading into battle.

All day long the fight raged, and not until four o'clock that afternoon did the two fleets part company. The slaughter on the Spanish decks was appalling, as the nimble English terrorized the invincible Armada, using the wind as their servant and not, as in the case of the Spanish, their master. The mangled Armada bravely reformed itself, in its customary half-moon formation. The English fleet stood off, confident that it could, at will, humble the might of Spain. The English casualties had been light – not a single ship had been lost. It was extraordinary.

That night, Howard wrote again to Walsingham, pleading for powder, shot and victuals: 'Ever since morning we have chased them in fight until this evening late and distressed them much; but their fleet consisteth of mighty ships and great strength ... and yet we pluck their feathers, little and little.' Howard estimated that three Spanish galleons had been sunk, and a further four had been put permanently out of action. For once a great commander in battle was not overestimating his success. Yet neither Howard, nor Drake, realized that the battle was over. The Armada was a spent force. As the blood red of a stormy sunset fired the western skies that evening, the English fleet watched, wearily as, in the distance, the vanquished Armada limped away, broken, towards the mud banks of Flanders. The elements themselves were now ready to provide the mortal blow.

Ark Royal

White Bear

Howard's flagship and was with him when, Drake having turned aside, they almost sailed into the rearguard of the Spanish fleet.

Captained by Lord Edmund Sheffield, she returned to the Thames estuary, following the dispersal of the Armada, in parlous condition, with strained timbers and leaking planks. Her sailors, too, were in poor shape, with dysentery and typhus.

AIR

There are many references to the elements in Elizabethan literature. 'Blow, winds, and crack your cheeks, rage, blow', laments Shakespeare in *King Lear*. The Elizabethans took the notions and properties of the four elements very seriously. Even Drake, for example, believed that men like the mutinous Thomas Doughty were capable of conjuring up foul weather. The Armada seemed the embodiment of all four elements. Earth could be said to be represented by Philip of Spain, its virtual ruler; Water marked the route taken by the Armada itself; Fire was the cause of its dispersal; and Air, as we shall see, was responsible for its final destruction.

Medina Sidonia was seeking a miracle – and he found it. As the English fleet slid smoothly away late that Monday afternoon, willing to bide its time before making the kill, a sudden and violent squall descended. The wind began to roar from the north-west, and the Armada began to drift, uncontrollably, in the direction of the shallow, menacing sandbanks. Desperately, the Duke tried to avoid the hidden snags; exhausted crews struggled manfully with torn sails and tattered rigging to prevent what seemed an inevitable doom. The banks were rising up to greet them ... seven fathoms, six fathoms, five.... The greatest, the strongest force ever gathered in Christendom was at the mercy of the elements.

Early on Tuesday morning, the Duke believed that it would be impossible to save a single ship from foundering and breaking up on the shoals:

'as they must inevitably be driven by the north west wind on to the banks of Zeeland.' Yet, from this hopeless prospect, 'We were saved by the wind shifting by God's mercy to the south west, and the Armada was then able to steer a northerly

Elizabeth Sydenham, second wife of Drake.

Buckland Abbey – home of Sir Francis Drake.

WILLIAM CECIL, LORD BURGHLEY

'Truly, Sir Francis Drake is a fearful man to the King of Spain.' – BURGHLEY

Elizabeth's sagacious chief minister was a powerful figure behind the planning of England's defence against Spain and the counter-Reformation in England, particularly in the war of espionage. In 1570 he organized a secret police to detect plots against Elizabeth, and later was instrumental in overseeing the execution of Mary Queen of Scots. He had his agents everywhere and there was little that went on in the underworld of politics of which he was not kept informed. His methods were often brutal, but so were those of the powers he acted against. Elizabeth recognized his capacity for administrative detail, his incorruptibility, and his devotion to public duty, though he received little financial reward from her for all his services.

His son, Thomas, was among the scores of volunteer citizens who flocked to take part in the defence of England as the Armada appeared in the Channel.

William Cecil, First Baron Burghley – from a copy of a portrait by Gheeraerts, held at Buckland Abbey.

The Lᵈ Admirall Howard Knighting Thomas Howard, the Lord Sheffeild, Rogᵗ Townsend Iohn Hawkins, and Martin Forbisher for their good service

Another in the series of playing cards, this one depicting Lord Howard knighting Hawkyns and Frobisher.

course. The wind from the SSW kept increasing in violence, and we continued to get further out to sea.' Modern-day meteorologists ascribe the sudden change of wind to the passage eastwards of a sharp ridge of high pressure ahead of an advancing low. Such jargon is now commonplace, but to the sixteenth century Spanish mind, this deliverance could mean only Divine intervention. It was the eve of St Lawrence, San Lorenzo. Did not their monarch worship with the monks of San Lorenzo in the chapel inside the Escorial? It was the answer to their prayer – 'The greater the difficulties,' they ought to have recalled to mind, 'the greater the favours of God.'

As the Armada swung away to the safety of deep water and the North Sea, the English watched with incredulity and frustration. The quarry fled, and its pursuers could do nothing to prevent it since they were, by now, completely out of ammunition. The Armada though, had been humbled: it was a beaten force. The *Maria Juan* had gone to the bottom together with one of the large, armed merchantmen. The *San Mateo* and the *San Felipe* had been snapped up by Justin of Nassau's flyboats, waiting like hungry sharks off the Dutch coast.

Not to be cheated, Howard set off in dogged pursuit of the fleeing Armada, putting on a 'brag countenance', as he described it, for he had nothing left with which to fight. The great Armada was, in fact, running away from empty guns.

Seymour, to his exasperated fury, was sent back to guard the approaches to the Thames, lest Parma should sneak forth. But Parma dared not emerge into the open sea. He realized that the Dutch would have annihilated his 17 000 troops in their flimsy, flat-bottomed landing craft. Seymour did not appreciate the strength of the Dutch allies, nor did Drake, who wanted a 'great eye' kept upon Parma. The wind bore the ragged tatters of a once great fleet northwards. It caused Drake to remark that the Spanish might soon attempt to bribe the King of Denmark: 'What the King of Spain's hot crowns will do in cold countries for mariners and men I leave to your Lordship [Walsingham] to judge.'

And then, in a phrase which cuts through the fog of time itself – a phrase which must have helped inspire a poet – Drake concluded his letter with the words 'But now half-sleeping – Fra: Drake'. So he was human after all. Perhaps he dreamed that night of the sequestered peace of Buckland Abbey, his Devon home.

As the southerlies bore the Armada to safety, Medina Sidonia assessed his losses. At least 3000 sick, an indeterminate number dead, and victuals remaining which might last a month, no more. At least 600 Spanish were killed at Gravelines, and 800 badly wounded. The way home was as tortuous as it was unknown and dangerous – around the north of Scotland, out into the Atlantic and due south, past Ireland. It looked reasonable enough on their maps, except their maps indicated a remarkably flat west coast of Ireland, with few, if any, of the physical projections which exist. The Duke was already framing excuses to the King for the flight of the Armada: 'My first duty seemed to save it. . .'.

Abreast of Lowestoft, on 31 July, with Seymour and Wynter having turned back for Harwich, Howard pressed on. Within the Armada it had been decided to make an example of those captains who, allegedly, had allowed their ships to drift out of action. Avila, captain of the *Santa Barbara*, was hanged. It was a vain attempt as much to expiate the disgrace as to confer a stricter sense of discipline. How the Duke must have resented the black looks and insults which now greeted him and the disagreeable martinet, Diego Flores. The more so since it appears that Medina Sidonia personally was not responsible for the act of barbarism.

At noon on Friday 2 August, north of Newcastle, the Spanish saw the last of the English ships disappear from the horizon astern.

The mood in the Spanish fleet was one of despair and ignominy. The military began a vendetta against the sea captains, which augured ill for the long voyage ahead. Medina Sidonia was obliged to introduce food rationing. It was little better than a starvation diet – half a pound of biscuit daily, half a pint of wine and a pint of water. To save water, they threw the animals overboard. A neutral merchant ship, crossing in the Armada's wake, reported a sea full of animals, mules and horses, still swimming.

From the wholesome air of his mountain fortress of the Escorial, Philip, totally unaware of what had occurred, and of the peril which his fleet now faced, wrote more despatches to the Duke of Medina Sidonia. In a letter penned on the night of the fireships, the King urged him to occupy the Thames and oblige the English army to split its forces on the two river banks. On 8 August, he wrote again, to congratulate the Duke upon his great victory in the English Channel! Neither letter reached its destination. Yet long after the Armada had miraculously been wafted clear by the wind from the Flanders coastline, reports of a victory over the English, and the death or capture of Drake, continued to reach Spain. Any other result was unthinkable, unimaginable. All Europe sighed in despair at these false reports – even most Catholics found Philip unbearable. The Pope resolutely refused to pay out the million ducats which he had promised until he had proof positive of a Spanish landing on English soil.

The Armada was fast vanishing from sight, pushed north into the cold and lonely seas by the gathering force of the wind. From the surviving personal diaries we may, with imagination, labour with the Armada when, on days beneath full sails and upon a heaving, rolling sea Medina Sidonia committed his thoughts to paper. The rationing of food scarcely affected him. Reading between the lines it becomes clear that he was suffering from sea-sickness, as he said he would. This was a man of considerable charity, even when others wallowed in the bitter taste of defeat. We learn, for example, that he gave one of his two warm sea cloaks to an ill-equipped priest, and the other to cover the body of a wounded cabin boy. Such a man ill-deserved what fate still had in store.

On Saturday 3 August, a great storm struck the Armada. The foul weather showed no sign of relenting. It was off Cape Wrath that the fleet began, literally, to break up, as the wooden planking, battered by shot and tempest, fell apart. The crew, more accustomed as were their ships to the calmer waters of the Mediterranean than the stippled green fury of the wind-whipped Outer Hebrides and Orkney, formed human chains to bail out the water from the holds. Yet many ships foundered on the wild Scottish coast.

The remains of the Armada turned south finally, heading down the coast of Ireland, which was itself then a rebellious country experiencing its own acute famine. A few years earlier, the rebels had been ruthlessly dealt with by the English, who now ruled from small, scattered garrisons. It was said, viciously, of the rebels, that 'like anatomies of death they did eat dead carrion and each other.' The Irish and the English have blamed each other for what happened to the wretched shipwrecked mariners washed ashore on Erin. It seems that Irishmen in English pay behaved with utter ruthlessness: one, Melaghlin

A medal struck after the Armada's 'dispersal': 'God blew and they were scattered'.

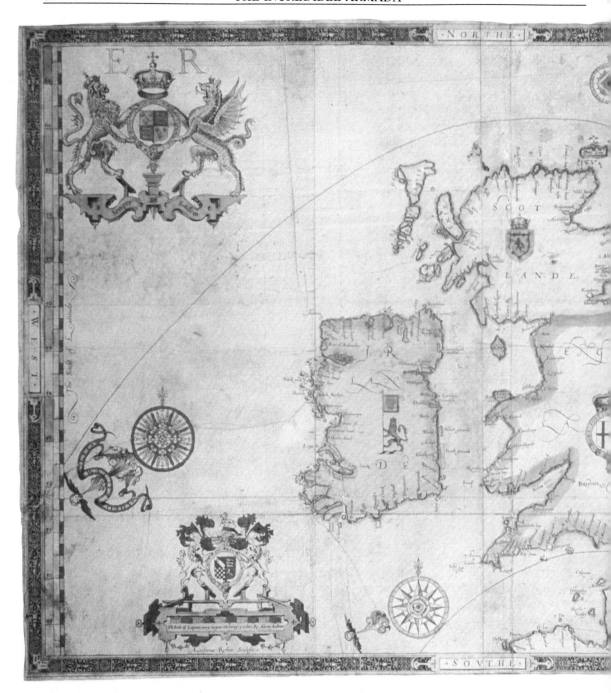

McCabb by name, is said to have slaughtered eighty helpless Spaniards with an axe. Other survivors were treated less harshly, some being held for ransom eventually returning to Spain.

The fate of the Armada on that forlorn and misty remote western shore is now almost lost in a sodden mixture of fact and fiction. Upon Donegal and Sligo, County Mayo and lovely Galway, through Clare, Kerry and Cork, the Armada's great back was finally broken. Some 6000 met their deaths from shipwreck, many in the most mournful and abhorrent circumstances in that frightful late summer. In the 1960s a gold ring was recovered from the wreck of the galleass *Girona*. It bore a young lover's promise in words which are heart-breaking in their poignancy: *'No*

tengo mas que dar te – I have nothing more to give thee.'

Medina Sidonia struggled home to Laredo, more dead than alive, on 12 September. He had to be carried to land. He never wanted to see the *San Martin* or the sea ever again. About fifty ships of his ragged fleet followed him in to the northern ports of Spain, their crews dying of starvation or of flux and fever, scurvy, typhus and influenza. At least one, a hospital ship, had circumnavigated the British Isles and ran up Channel again, in the hope of finding a friendly haven in France. She foundered, off Bolt Tail, in South Devon.

The ships were as broken as the men. From his sick bed, the Duke fretted for his crews,

The route of the 'Invincible Armada' around the coast of England, Scotland and Ireland, and the path taken by the defeated ships as they made for home.

some 20 000 perished. David Howarth, in his excellent account of the Spanish side of this epic saga, estimates that 1500 died in battle, 6000 in shipwrecks, 1000 by murder, judicial and otherwise, and the rest from starvation and disease.

The Armada crews blamed the Duke of Parma more than any other individual for this great human disaster. No one dared blame the King, of course, since kings were divinely appointed. Philip received the defeat with the same stoic impassivity as he had received news of the great Spanish victory at Lepanto, years earlier. The Armada had sailed in the name of God – to question the Almighty's judgment now, or to betray any emotional response including, worst of all, pity, would be to imply that the Divine was less than perfect. That would have been, to Philip's way of thinking, an act of betrayal, of heresy. The bigot. Thrice again this aged, gouty recluse, planning his wargames during nightly vigils in his cramped quarters in the Escorial, launched further Armadas against England. To no avail. Only one, off Falmouth in Cornwall in 1597, almost succeeded. It was beaten back, ironically, by yet another gale – on this occasion from the winds of the north.

Before he died, in 1598, Philip had threatened one reluctant captain-general of an Armada that if he did not comply immediately with the royal command he would have him hung around the neck of his wife. Blind fanaticism combined with the cruelty of the Inquisition. Little wonder the English fought for their lives. But the English too had problems. In the short-term, their grateful deliverance was tempered with worries that the Armada might return to the attack. Drake, in particular, counselled caution. Howard, having seen the enemy past the Firth of Forth, sped south to tend conscientiously and compassionately to the diseases now ravaging his men: 'It is a thing that ever followeth such great sarvyses,' he wrote. Seymour was posted to watch the eastern coast of England, Grenville to the west.

Burghley, the Lord Treasurer, convinced himself that the Armada would not return, while Elizabeth, 'not a whit dismayed' despite the critical months her kingdom had endured, went down to the city in state, to give thanks at St Paul's. It was 8 September, and the Queen was received with unfeigned joy by her subjects. Eleven Armada ensigns, or banners, later hung on London Bridge, were displayed at Paul's Cross. It was, as the outstanding Elizabethan scholar of our own times, the Cornishman, Dr A.L. Rowse tells us, 'like her coronation all over

thinking only of their plight in the squalid, stinking hulks. He blamed only himself for the calamity. Finally, they placed him in a curtained, horse-drawn litter, and sent him and what remained of his servants home, over the mountains, to the cool peace of his beloved San Lucar. The wounds of defeat never left this melancholy man long into his old age. Philip excused him the duty and privilege of coming to court to kiss hands – as he excused himself the boredom and indignity of visiting the vanquished Armada, the fleet whose doom was his responsibility. It was more than enough that at least a third and probably nearer a half, of the 130 ships which set sail never returned to Spain. It is also probable that of the 30 000 or so men who made up the Armada, again, with all the streets hung with blue stammel'. The bells pealed joyfully, not in alarm as it was intended they should had the Armada landed.

Elizabeth's feelings of jubilation were clouded with sorrow. Leicester, her adored companion and kinsman, her trusty liegeman was dead. 'His last letter,' she wrote, as she folded it away. But there was little time for grief. Her tears of sadness turned to joy as the news from Ireland came in. '*Flavit Jehovah et dissipati sunt* – God blew, and they were scattered' ran the inscription on the Armada medals struck at the time.

Not that the great Architect of the Universe drew much distinction between the disease visited upon Catholic and Protestant survivors of the Armada campaign. Howard was aghast at what he now witnessed: 'Sickness and mortality begins wonderfully to grow amongst us; and it is a most pitiful sight to see, here at Margate, how the men, having no place to receive them into here, die in the streets. It would grieve any man's heart to see them that have served so valiantly to die so miserably.'

But Burghley and the Queen were at their wits' end for cash. We can almost catch the sound of Burghley's quill, hear him suck through his teeth as he replied to Howard, calming the outrage at such seeming injustice. Poor Howard, having been hounded in the closing days of the Armada by bureaucratic interference, now found himself the subject of a whispering campaign – that he ought to have engaged the enemy, taken more prize money. Howard, furious at the neglect of his men, raided Don Pedro's golden hoard stowed on Drake's *Revenge*, and pawned his own plate to pay for the cost of their care. Drake turned a Nelsonian eye on his commander's activities. All Howard kept from the famous victory was all he asked for – the banner from the captured *Rosario*.

Even the gentle Sir John Hawkyns had yet to contend with a series of hare-brained accusations about the condition of the Queen's ships. Frobisher, conspicuously absent from Howard's final Council of War, grumbled on about Drake. However, Drake was making for Plymouth – away from the quarrels, far from the intrigue and gossip of Court. To Plymouth where, it was said, the Mayors were as independent and unconstrained in their dealings as the Doges of Venice themselves. In Cattedown harbour he saw the good ship *Elizabeth Jonas*, so christened by the Queen early in her reign because she had been reminded how, like the prophet Jonas, she too had been delivered from her enemies. The ship was rife with disease, and the locals were trying to cleanse her of infection 'with fires of wet broom'. The famous Black Book of Plymouth had recorded the Armada thus: 'Godd be prased the enymye hadd never power to land somoche as one manne uppon any territorie of ours.' The spelling is strange, but the sentiment fitted perfectly with the mood of the nation.

Queen Elizabeth, who had celebrated her fifty-fifth birthday on 7 September, was as untiring as ever, despite her three full decades on the throne. She forsook Hampton Court for Richmond that Christmas. Burghley gave her a massive present of gold plate engraved with symbols of her Armada triumph. To Howard, he presented a sarsenet, a fine soft fabric, decorated with rubies, diamonds and pearls. The Court discussed the coming year's campaigns, in which Drake's name figured large. War with Spain was to continue until the end of Elizabeth's reign, in 1603.

The old warhorse, Frobisher, died in Plymouth of all places, in January 1595. Later that year, in November, the ever-loyal Sir John Hawkyns perished at sea during a joint and disastrous expedition with Drake. That genius of the oceans himself died just seventy-seven days later. Both men, who dreamed of bringing the empire of Spain to its knees, were buried at sea. The great water accepted these immortals as its own. Drake died dressed in armour – a dying wish: Hawkyns, still conscience-striken about the failure of the voyage, in his will left £2000 to the Queen, to sweeten Gloriana's memories of him.

The defeat of the Armada was a milestone in history. The English success had stemmed the advance of the Counter-Reformation in Europe, allowing the emerging Protestant states – Sweden, Germany, Holland – to feel free to make up their minds what form of religion they should have. Yet it was to take a bloody fight lasting well

Drake's lodestone – used to magnetize the ship's compass needle.

into the next century before man realized that, with toleration, two ideologies could co-exist in reasonable harmony.

The Armada was a great victory if only because it raised the hearts of men in dark hours. It was the stuff of dreams and legends more important, perhaps, than the actual events themselves. England, which had now found a place in the sun, began the long journey towards maturity and unity of purpose. The irresistible impulse was to expand, and future centuries were to witness what this small nation was capable of – and still is. 'There must be a beginning of any great matter,'

Drake had written, from his ocean realm, 'but the continuing of the same to the end until it be thoroughly finished yieldeth the true glory.'

Such inspiration those Elizabethans of yesteryear provide for us. The distinguished master historian, G.M. Trevelyan, summed it up for ever when he wrote that 'once on this earth, once, on this familiar spot of ground, walked other men and women as actual as we are today.' Thinking their own thoughts, swayed by their own passions, but now all gone, one generation vanishing after another, gone as utterly as we ourselves shall surely be gone. Like ghosts at cockcrow.

The sublime 'Virgin Queen', on a commemorative medal.

Principal sources of information were:

Black, J.B.	The Reign of Queen Elizabeth
Bryant, Arthur	The Elizabethan Deliverance
Corbett, J.S.	Drake and the Tudor Navy
Garin, Eugenio	Astrology in the Renaissance
Howarth, David	The Voyage of the Armada: The Spanish Story
Laughton, J.K.	State Papers Relating to the Defeat of the Spanish Armada
Mattingly, Garrett	The Defeat of the Spanish Armada
McKee, Alexander	From Merciless Invaders
Rowse, A.L.	Sir Richard Grenville of the Revenge and The Expansion of Elizabethan England
Tillyard, E.M.W.	The Elizabethan World Picture
Usherwood, S.	The Great Enterprise – The History of the Spanish Armada
Williamson, J.A.	Hawkins of Plymouth and The Age of Drake
Youings, Joyce	Sixteenth Century England

together with numerous articles from The Mariner's Mirror, The Transactions of the Devonshire Association and the University of East Anglia publication, A Meteorological Study: the Spanish Armada Storms.

A romanticized view of Drake's funeral. Burial at Sea by Thomas Davidson.

Drake's personal flags. The star symbol is also shown on his family's arms.